**NATIONAL
GEOGRAPHIC**

Count the Animals

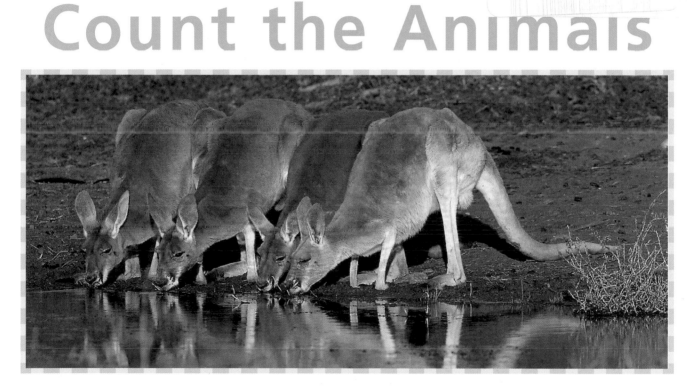

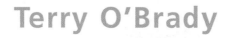

Terry O'Brady

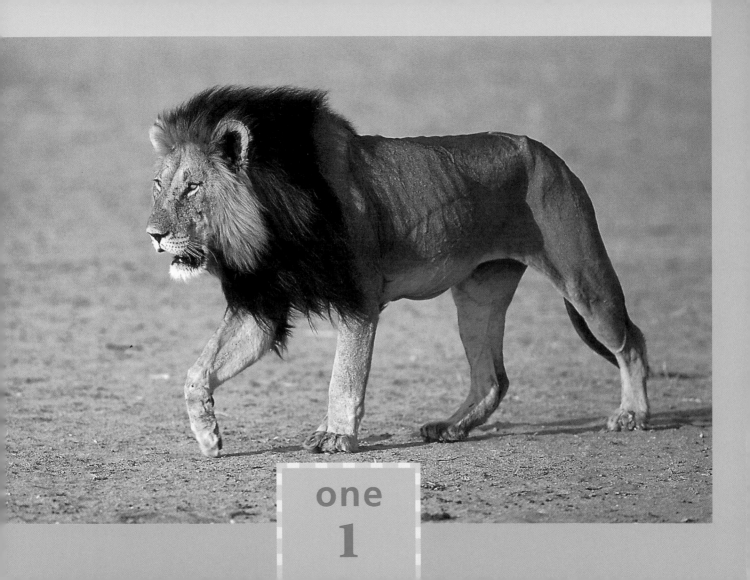

one
1

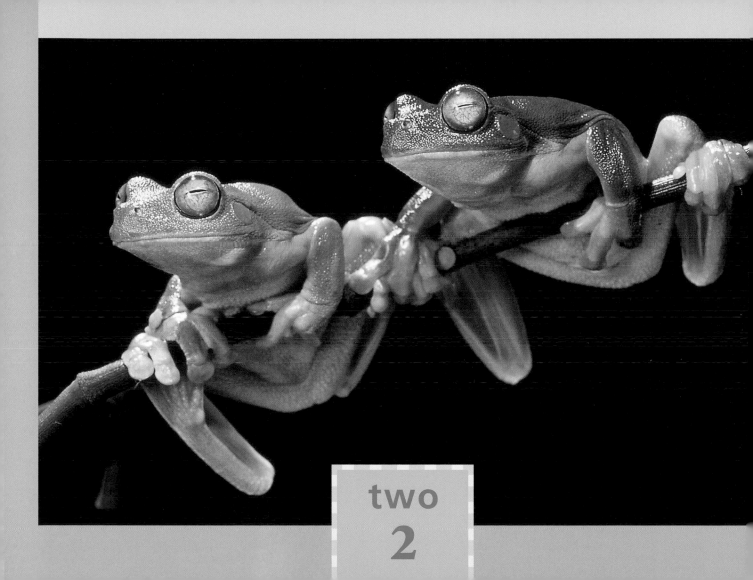

two
2

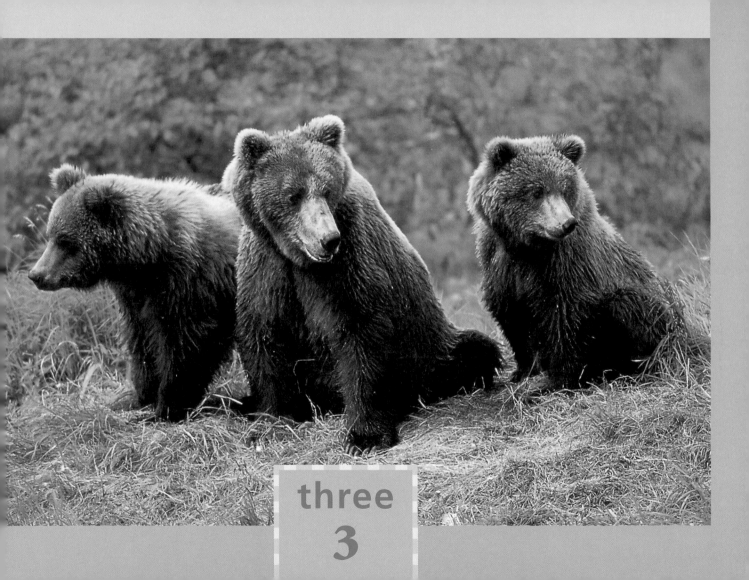

three
3

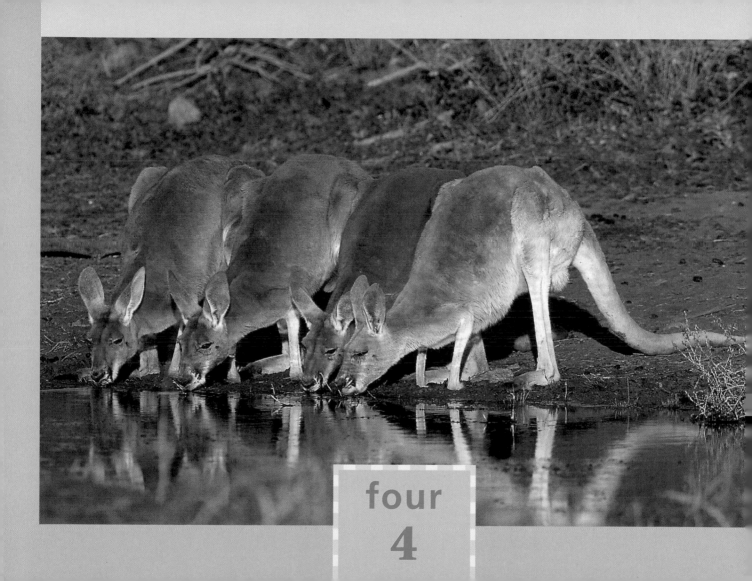

four
4

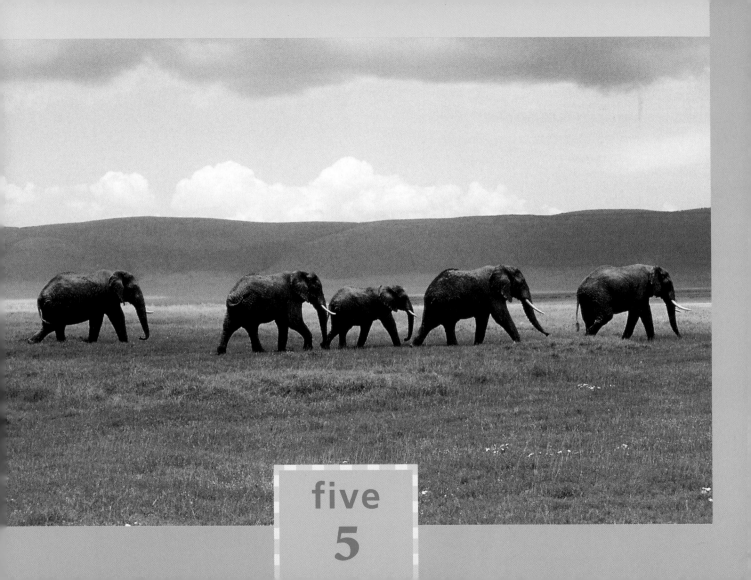

five

5

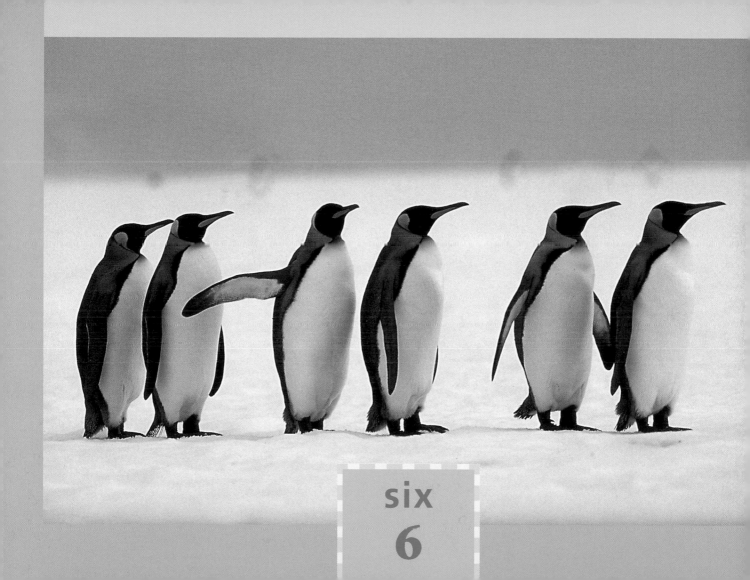

six

6

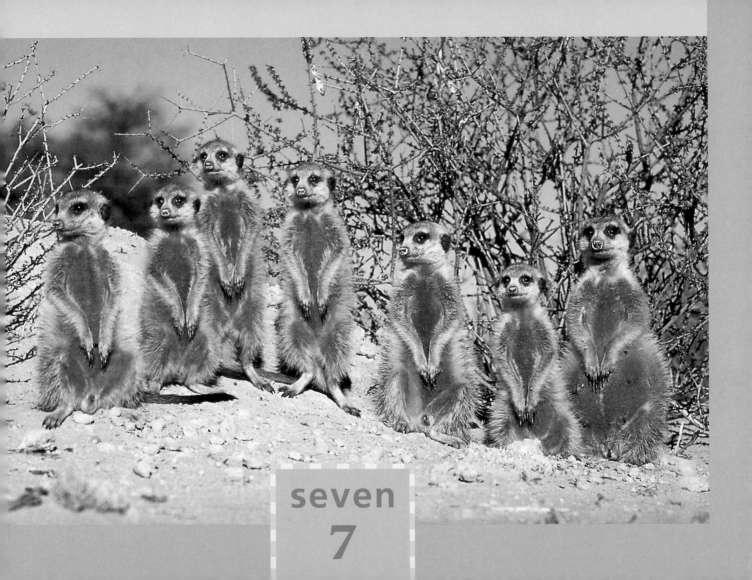

seven
7

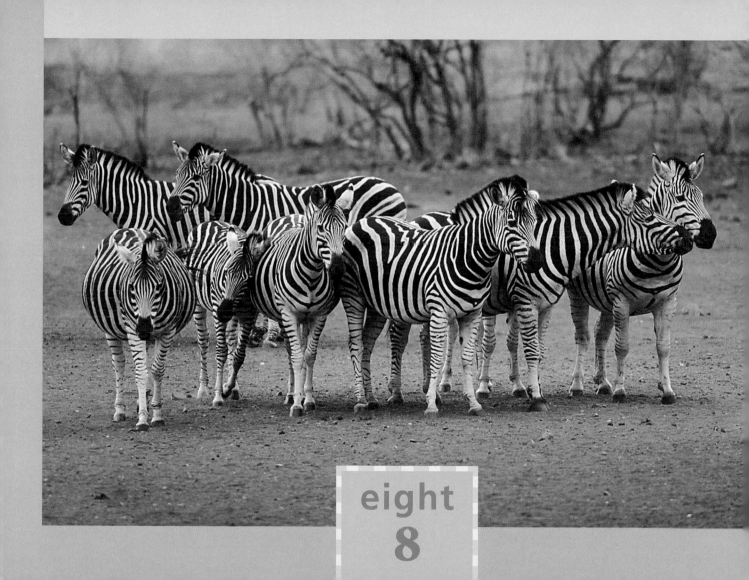

eight
8

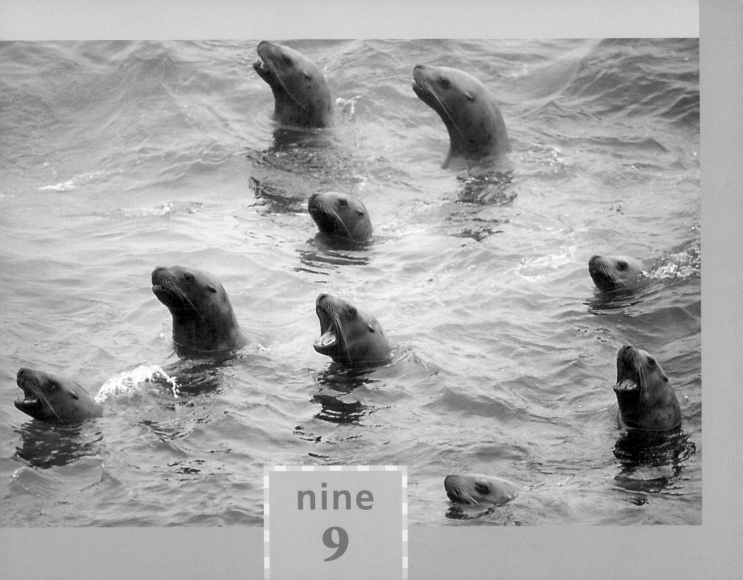

nine
9

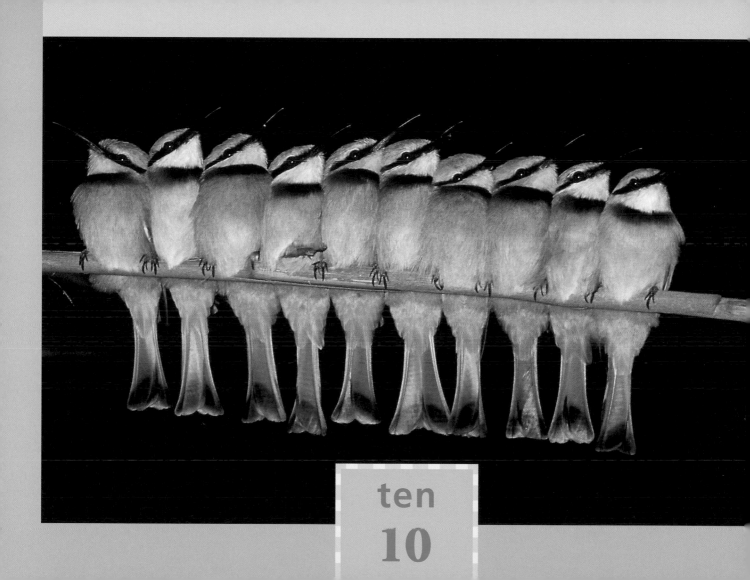

ten

10

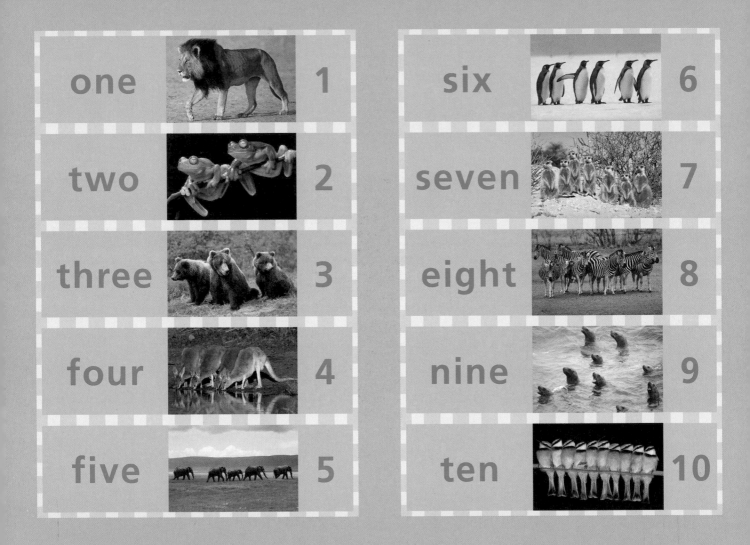

one		1
two		2
three		3
four		4
five		5
six		6
seven		7
eight		8
nine		9
ten		10